FENG SHUI

THIS IS A CARLTON BOOK

Text and Design © Carlton Books Limited, 1999

This edition published by Carlton Books Limited, 1999

A CIP catalogue record for this book is available from the British Library

ISBN 1 85868 762 4

Project Editor: Camilla MacWhannell
Project art direction: Adam Wright
Design and Editorial: Paul Middleton & Warren Lapworth
Production: Garry Lewis
Picture Research: Alex Pepper
Feng shui expert: Rénuka

Printed and bound in Dubai

FENG SHUI

A Practical Guide
to Health, Wealth
and Happiness

KAREN
FARRINGTON

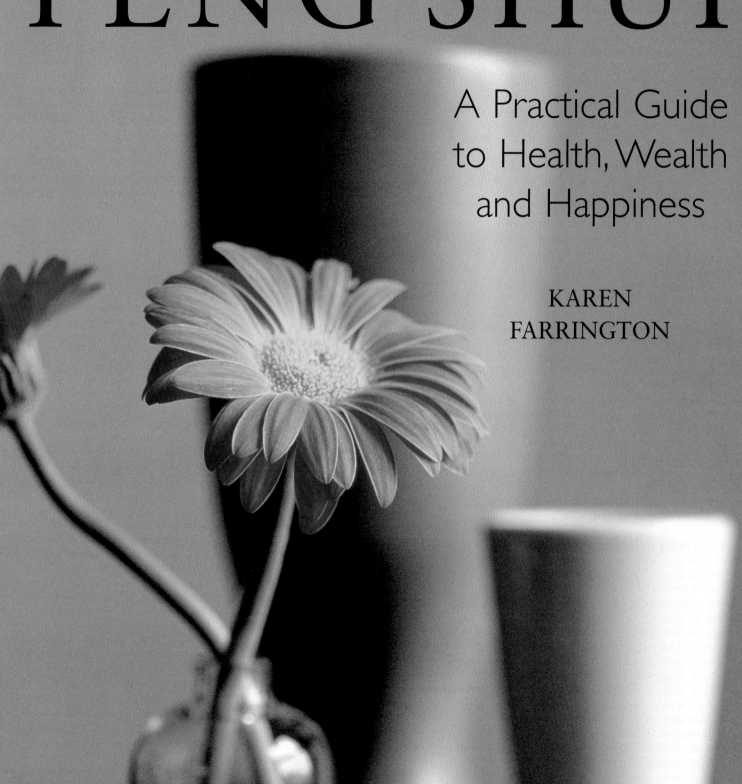

CARLTON

CONTENTS

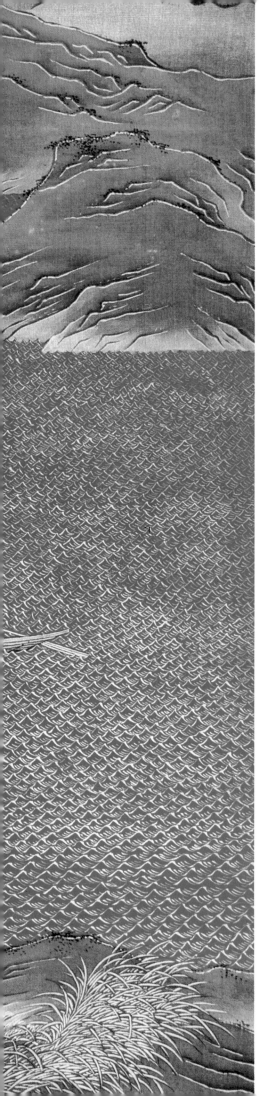

INTRODUCTION

In our mind's eye, we prefer to picture ourselves gliding through life, imbued with inner peace and at one with the world. The choices we make are wise ones, the luck we receive constant and the fortunes we accrue long lasting. Ambitions such as these are by no means the preserve of the modern age. It was this pursuit of harmony and sensory well-being that, centuries ago, led to the founding of feng shui.

Commonly, it is believed to be the art of placement — switching a vase from one side of the room to the other and changing the angle of the sofa. Placement is an important aspect of feng shui but the subject is three dimensional — broad, long and extremely deep. There's intuition, astrology, understanding the elements, moral fortitude, design, horticulture, aquaculture and much more. Just as you comprehend a face of feng shui, an entirely different one presents itself. With feng shui, one is looking for clues and putting together pieces of evidence to get a full picture.

In translation, feng means 'wind' and shui means 'water'; it is pronounced *foong shway* in southern China, *foong shay* in northern China. Immediately it is cast into the realms of wild nature, but these days it applies just as well to towns and cities. Through feng shui, forces which are both natural and invisible are tamed and even exploited. It is a question of striving to achieve balance in the immediate environment.

Feng shui is a way of life in many Eastern countries. In Hong Kong, for example, ninety per cent of businesses employ feng shui consultants as a matter of course. It is also in vogue in the West, an irresistible lure for the rich, famous, urban, New Age and incurably curious. Among those who profess an interest are American tycoon Donald Trump, British entrepreneur Richard Branson and the international banking giants HSBC.

This book doesn't have all the answers — none could. It's a glimpse at an immense subject and is designed to give a new perspective on a practice that counts its age in millennia.

HISTORY AND PRINCIPLES

Feng shui is not the work of one man but of many. It started with the thoughts and findings of an elite few, hundreds of years BC. However, different layers have been added down the centuries which have combined to form the complex Eastern art which we see today. Alas, much of the history of feng shui has been lost in the mist of time. Still we can detect the important influences in its growth, which were Taoism, Chinese astrology, divination skills and local religious beliefs. Everyone is eager to get on with the business of feng shui. First, though, glimpse its grass roots and get a feel for the principles that govern it. There is much to learn. After reading this book there will still remain acres of information unspecified. This is, after all, only a brief clip taken from an epic movie, the beginning of a journey which could take a lifetime to complete. Don't be daunted. In common with most topics, nobody has to be an expert to feel the benefits of feng shui by taking the first, faltering steps. Treat those who claim otherwise with healthy suspicion. Modern feng shui is no longer based in superstition. If your first instincts spoke of incense, spirits and self-styled holy men, toss them aside. There are no rituals and there's definitely no magic involved. Still, it remains a challenge for rational Western minds to grapple with inscrutable oriental philosophies (would the new job/windfall/relationship claimed as a result of feng shui have occurred anyway?). Only the most arrogant would condemn centuries of Chinese wisdom without a second thought. Sample some basic concepts before coming to your own conclusions.

Tao and I Ching

Before delving into the history of feng shui, it is essential to assume an Oriental perspective on life and its abundant mythology, superstition and religion.

Chief among the Chinese faiths is Taoism, which has been one of the most profound influences on feng shui. Lao Tzu, 'the hidden sage', is thought to have lived in the sixth century BC – although he may never have lived at all, the words attributed to him being the collected works of many authors. He is the shadowy figure held responsible for the Tao faith and the alleged author of Tao Teh Ching, its major text. His words are enigmatic, for it was never his intention to lecture in Tao; rather to lead followers along a path down which they would experience enlightenment for themselves.

Tao – pronounced *dow* – translates to 'the way' or sometimes 'the universe' and is linked to peace, meditation, naturalness and serenity. It is passive, spontaneous and flows freely. Tao is a tangle for those Westerners with narrow thought processes and deeply entrenched ideas. Confucianism may be more appealing, with its easily understood

W: Alexander f

London Published Oct.ʳ 19. 1800. by G & W. Nicol Pall mall.

RIGHT: Lao Tzu – 'The teaching without speaking and the benefits of not-doing are only rarely found in the world.'

hierarchical notions. Confucius (551-479 BC) was a scholarly man who sought a post as advisor at the emperor's court, but his ambitions were constantly thwarted. Instead, he became a teacher and writer. He taught the importance of propriety, duty and manners, and advocated a strong moral code, as well as the need for charity and fraternal love. Confucius embraced the *I Ching* or 'Book of Changes', a system of Chinese wisdom developed in about 2852 BC by Emperor Fu-hsi, who is said to have discovered the fundamental eight symbols or trigrams (three horizontal lines in parallel) on the back of a sacred tortoise. Each symbol comprises three lines, either complete or broken. King Wen expanded the system in 1143 BC. He paired the symbols and discovered there were then 64 possible combinations of the six lines. I Ching – also known as Yijing – works on the premise that there is no such thing as chance. As people seek the advice of the hexagrams, either by tossing coins or yarrow sticks, destiny takes a hand. The pattern of the hexagrams and the order in which they appear is 'meant' and an interpreter using his finely tuned powers of intuition can read it.

ABOVE: 'Life and death are one, right and wrong are the same,' according to Tao scholar Chuang Tzu (350-275 BC).

LEFT: Among the verdant hills of ancient China Taoism flourished and out of this enigmatic faith came feng shui.

Form School

Although the date which marks the origin of feng shui is unknown – 4000 BC is a ball-park figure – its purpose was almost certainly to divine auspicious burial sites for emperors. Like most cultures of that distant era, great ceremony was made in committing an earthly ruler to what was presumed to be an opulent afterlife. In China the veneration of ancestors has always been a particularly important custom.

BELOW: The father of the Form School of feng shui was Yang Yun Sang who committed its principles to parchment.

The talents of the feng shui masters were also put to good use in siting palaces. Soon a well-chosen location was thought to make the difference between a lengthy, peaceful reign and a short, squalid one. Masters spoke in animal metaphors, using beasts of special significance to the Chinese, but they were mainly driven by topology. Their first concern was to distinguish the green dragon, or a range of verdant hills, in the east or to the left of the proposed site. The undulating spine of the imaginary dragon would fit snugly beneath the line of the hilltops. In the west there would be the white tiger, with its lower profile. Ideally the forms would curve in a horseshoe configuration and the spot where dragon and tiger consummate their relationship was the most appropriate for building. It meant all imperial tombs were built in the scenic shelter of hill ranges. In addition there would be a tortoise, or hill, to the rear and red phoenix to the fore. As the prosperous Tang dynasty fell into disarray in the last years of the ninth century, Form feng shui – otherwise known as the Kanchow method, Kwang Hsi School, Kiangsi method and the Shapes School – was elevated to new heights. The cultural wealth that had been a hallmark of the Tang dynasty was in rapid decline. Buddhism, always a vital religious influence in China, had been diagnosed a disruptive force and thousands of monks and nuns were being hounded. Against this turbulent background it was royal advisor Yang Yun Sang in the Kwangsi province who refined the basics of feng shui and committed them to parchment. If he was seeking a return to the halcyon days of the Tang dynasty, when epic poetry and ceramics, art and sculpture were dominant, Yang Yun Sang was to be disappointed. But if his aim was to bring back an element of spirituality to a country obsessed with Confucian-style civil discipline, he was an unqualified success. He is best remembered for Han Luang Ching ('Art of Rousing the Dragon'), while two further books gave pointers on how to find the dragon's lair and how to locate the dragon in flatter regions. The scripts he wrote became trail-blazing classics and were the hub of feng shui during the ensuing centuries.

The Great Wall of China, dating from around 200 years BC, is viewed as an engineering triumph. Yet its main architect, Meng Tian, bitterly regretted his life's work. Built to keep Chinese farmers in and nomads from the north out, the wall followed river courses, mountainsides and valleys, in keeping with the wisdom of feng shui. But before he was tricked into committing suicide (believing his death was called for by royal command), Meng Tian wrote: 'I have made walls and ditches over more than 10,000 li [a Chinese measurement equivalent to about 1,200 miles]. In this distance it is impossible not to have cut through the veins of the earth. I have a crime for which to die.'

BELOW: The Great Wall of China was deemed by its designer to have 'cut the veins of the earth', and he was prepared to die for his supposed crime.

Compass School

Master Sang was the inspiration for the scholar Wang Chih who, in the subsequent Song dynasty, developed the art of Compass feng shui. Chih was clearly a practical man, for he saw that Form feng shui could not be applied convincingly to the region around his home in the southeastern plains of China, where mountains (or dragons) were few. So around the 10th century, Sang strived to create the far more detailed Compass method of feng shui, also known as the Ancestral Hall method and the Fukien and Min schools. This relies more on detailed celestial influences than merely landscape.

BELOW: Dragons have been key mythological figures in China since earliest times.

Later still, a government official by the name of Cun Guan abandoned his job in order to tour the regions and gather further evidential weight in favour of Compass feng shui. Thousands of sites were catalogued for the purposes of feng shui, even in those early years. It was his detailed examinations that led to refinements such as the Eight House system and the Triple Gate system, which will be explained later on.

It was in the Compass school of feng shui that I Ching became particularly relevant. The I Ching symbols are among the many which appear

around the feng shui compass. It can have as many as 36 rings, each with between eight and 365 segments. The readings are painstaking and complicated but always precise. In short, the compass can be applied to properties to discover information personal to the enquirer.

Today, little distinction is made between the two principle schools of feng shui, or indeed the minor branches of the art, like Water feng shui, which has been practised since 600 AD. Most practitioners appear to favour Compass feng shui, as it offers lavish detail and increased potential, but the rules of the Form school aren't overlooked, though they may appear obsolete at first. Tall buildings have been substituted for mountains, rivers replaced by busy roads. The physical demands of the Form school remain sound. A workable hybrid has evolved.

OPPOSITE, BELOW: *Feng shui compasses are detailed and difficult to comprehend without study.*

LEFT: *Important buildings in Hong Kong are designed in accordance with advice from feng shui masters.*

Ch'i and Poison Arrows

Fundamental to feng shui is ch'i. It is sometimes called cosmic breath, dragon's breath or universal life force. Its literal translation is breath, gas or ether, but it means much more than merely hot air. In layman's terms it means streams of energy.

Feng shui and acupuncture share a common ancestry. Both were developed in China thousands of years ago and ch'i is central to both. Acupuncturists insert needles at various points in the body with a view to manipulating ch'i as it courses along pathways inside the body known as meridians. So ch'i is both in the body, rotating much as blood does, and it also surges across the earth, waiting to be harnessed. The Chinese are not alone in their concept of earth energy. Hindus know it as Prana which, they say, pervades all forms of life. In Japan the term is 'ki' and, with the advent of the samurai, it became a crucial discipline for warriors representing courage, willpower, and spiritual and moral strength. It remains relevant today in the many forms of Japanese martial arts. Hawaiians acquainted with Huna, the island's traditional esoteric philosophy, call this kind of earth energy 'mana'. But ch'i can be dispersed, blown away or even flushed down the toilet. Windy sites are useless at gathering ch'i, as are steep slopes, where ch'i can roll away. And while it should not flow too rapidly, nor should it stagnate. The aim is to accumulate friendly, meandering ch'i,

ABOVE: Acupuncture and feng shui both endorse the theory that energy travels in invisible lines.

ABOVE: Long, straight roads, like this one in Arizona, USA, are considered poor feng shui.

thereby enhancing daily life, and the way to do that is through feng shui. It is not enough, however, to be concerned with ch'i and how to hold onto it. Feng shui is all about balance and assumes everything has an opposite. The flip side of ch'i is shar ch'i, or killing breath. This is the wrong kind of energy, which carries misfortune, bad luck and ill-health. It can be directed at you or your abode by poison arrows – sharp or angular objects pointing in your direction. How do you spot a poison arrow? Look for straight roads, canals, railway lines, a telegraph pole, pylon or aerial, satellite dishes, church spires, the corners of neighbouring buildings and similarly shaped objects. Few objects shaped like these occur naturally. Such was the fear of sharp-edged roofs that the builders of pagodas, which were first constructed in China more than 1,500 years ago, put upward-curving edges at gutter height to deflect shar ch'i from neighbouring homes.

ABOVE: Pagodas were designed with upward-pointing roof edges to channel negative energy away from neighbours.

Yin and Yang and the Eight Trigrams

Most people are familiar with the Yin and Yang symbol, one of the all time triumphs of graphic design. It so ably expresses balance and interaction, an equation that is vital to the understanding and practise of feng shui.

The symbol is called the Tai Ji Tu or 'diagram of the supreme ultimate', with the white 'fish' representing Yang and the black representing Yin. Each has an eye in the opposing colour to demonstrate that all forces contain an iota of their opposite. Yin and Yang are contained in a circle – which symbolises unity – and ebb and flow in a perpetual cycle. The symbol can be used to represent humans who are thought of in Oriental philosophy as being light and dark. This does not mirror the good/evil constituents of human nature that are reflected in Christianity. The dark of Yin is not indicative of bad deeds, it is merely in opposition to the light of Yang and acts positively to provide a harmonious equilibrium. Through Yin and Yang the Chinese organise the world into categories.

The trigrams of the I Ching emerged from Yin and Yang imagery, with the unbroken line representing Yang and the broken, Yin.

According to the I Ching, 'the Great Primal Beginning' made two forces which generated four images. Out of those four images came the eight trigrams, around which Compass feng shui revolves. At the bottom of the pile is man; the middle line represents earth, with its seasons and compass directions; and at the top is heaven. It is the bottom line which lies nearest to the centre. Those three lines act as a shorthand note for the experienced feng shui practitioner, for each trigram has a host of associations, including element, time of day and season. It's a simple way of saying a lot. Remember, the Chinese do not ascribe to the theory of random selection. They

YIN	YANG
Passive	Active
Female	Male
Earth	Heaven
Dark	Bright
Water	Fiery
Yielding	Hard
Cold	Warm
North	South
Valleys	Hills
Hidden	Overt
Even numbers	Odd numbers
Light	Heavy
Rain	Sun

ABOVE: A coin with the trigram design made to mark New Year celebrations in China.

do, however, know three types of luck reflecting the trigrams, that from heaven – beyond human control – from earth, which is another way of expressing feng shui, and from man, improved by good conduct.

A summary of the eight trigrams is as follows:
- **Chienë:** The Creative, also linked to heaven, summer, white, father and the number six.
- **Kunë:** The Receptive, also linked to earth, winter, yellow, mother and the number two.
- **Chenë:** The Arousing, also linked to thunder, khaki, the eldest son and the number three.
- **Sunë:** The Gentle, also linked to wind, wood, green, the eldest daughter and the number four.
- **Tuië:** The Joyous, also linked to the lake, metal, silver, the youngest daughter and the number seven.
- **Kenë:** The Stillness, also linked to the mountain, earth, beige, the youngest son and the number eight.
- **Kanë:** The Abysmal, also linked to water, blue, the middle son and the number one.
- **Lië:** The Clinging, also linked to fire, red, the middle daughter and the number nine.

BELOW: Everything on earth and beyond is Yin or Yang. Practitioners can divine the identities of opposite forces.

The Five Elements

To predict the future, to assess and assist relationships, to appreciate a sense of self, it is necessary to grasp the Chinese system of five elements. These are categories into which people, places, planets, seasons and colours all fall. Each has different general traits; the twin talents of reflection and representation are key for interpretation.

The elements are fire, earth, metal, wood and water. Each is linked to a season, colour, a time of day and much more. For example, water – winter, black, old age; wood – spring, blue, birth; fire – summer, red, pre-pubescent; earth – late summer/early autumn, yellow, adolescent; metal – autumn, white, adulthood.

The mechanics of the elements and the relationships they have between one another are straightforward to visualise. Productively, water is the lifeblood of wood; without wood there would

BELOW: With roots breaking into the ground the wood element is said to destroy earth.

be no fire, with its warmth and light; fire produces earth, with its residue of ashes; metals means minerals and ores, found within the earth, and molten metal finds strength in water.

However, there's also a destructive cycle, with the roots of wood breaking up earth; earth damming the flow of water in rivers; water extinguishing fire; flames melting metal; and metal, moulded into an axe or saw, cutting wood down to size.

Being destructive need not necessarily be a bad thing, as far as feng shui goes. The aim, as ever, is to achieve a balance. If one element is dominating, to the detriment of the rest, it must be countered by the introduction of another which curbs it.

The elements correspond to a direction that is revealed on the feng shui compass. Landscapes have an element, with steep hills and round tops being wood, angular peaks representative of fire, broader, less bold summits are metal, hills with flat or plateaux tops are earth, and fluctuating tops associated with water.

ELEMENT	SEASON	COLOUR	TIME
Wood	Spring	Blue	Birth
Fire	Summer	Red	Pre-pubescent
Earth	Late summer /early autumn	Yellow	Adolescent
Metal	Autumn	White	Adulthood
Water	Winter	Black	Old Age

ABOVE: Fire is supported by wood but destroyed by water.

Pa Kua and the Feng Shui Compass

Its modern translation is 'bagua', but there's nothing up to date about the octagon that maps out the direction of the eight ancient trigrams. For the Chinese this is the essential symbol of feng shui and it has endured for centuries. There are two systems for setting down the trigrams on the pa kua.

One is the 5,000-year-old Early Heaven Sequence, in which Yin is aligned with the north and Yang the south and the elements are likewise logically positioned. It is this arrangement which is used for pa kua mirrors, more of which later. Then there is the Later Heaven Sequence, the legacy of King Wen, 2,000 years younger and developed particularly for use with the I Ching. It is generally felt to be more obscure but also more reliable for use in domestic dwellings. The feng shui compass, or lo p'an, extends considerably beyond the boundaries of the pa kua at its heart. The compass is awesomely complex with numerous rings rippling from the centre. Consider just how precise it can be. Taking a straight line from the centre to

RIGHT: Among the rings on a feng shui compass are those denoting elements, lucky sectors, directions and even time.

the outer circumference, one direction can align at least 17 and as many as 36 different symbols. It is the combination of these rings that is interpreted for a feng shui reading. There is phenomenal and specific detail here which is said to give feng shui its potency.

Among the rings that you may find on the compass are the heavenly stems – lucky and unlucky sectors – and the 12 earthly branches – indicative of direction, years, months and hours. It also includes the eight major planets, divisions of Yin and Yang, the five elements, the fortnights of the year, and more. Already you can see there's much more to talk about here than this book

allows. The Chinese direction of south is always found at the top of the compass, yet north at the bottom remains true north. This occurs because the Chinese find south to be a more auspicious direction, being sunny and warm. It is also the direction of Yang (upwards) and heaven. Don't forget to make this adjustment when you use a pa kua or lo p'an.

It's easy to apply the pa kua or lo p'an to your home. Simply map out the rooms and superimpose the pa kua with due regard to direction, then you will know which room falls into which sector. The pa kua can also be applied to individual rooms.

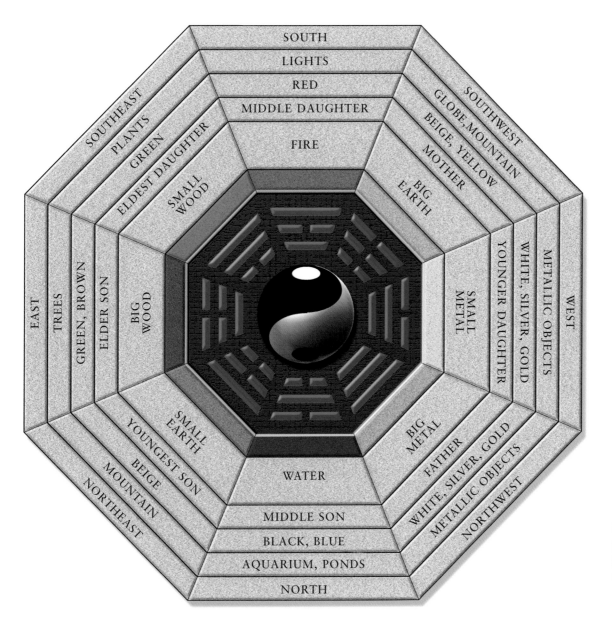

LEFT: South is always found at the top of the pa kua compass with its eight trigrams.

FENG SHUI FOR YOU

Feng shui has sustained its popularity not because hordes have become deeply engrossed in the message of ancient Chinese texts, but because it can be used in homes everywhere without recourse to complex theoretical debate. Its outcome is to boost levels of harmonious equilibrium in everyday life. Feng shui often states the obvious. The essence of a home with good feng shui is one that is clear of clutter. We all know how stressful it can be to live and work in a mess. Piles of laundry, collections of papers, shoes left strewn over the floor – all jobs crying out to be tackled. A disorganised house is often a symptom of a disorganised mind, one that is troubled by the tasks left undone and distracted from the matter in hand. This makes us feel weary and oppressed, disgruntled with our environment and ourselves. Following the sound advice offered by feng shui provides a cure by dealing with the original symptoms.

Dripping taps, noisy plumbing and squeaky doors are all factors for poor feng shui, which quickly play havoc on the nerves. Many of the improvements made by feng shui at this initial level can be instituted with minimum effort and money. It is impossible to grasp the finer techniques of feng shui in a do-it-yourself manual – to imagine that one can simply tap into wisdom that's been gathered over centuries is a naïve notion. But the questions in this section are likely to echo those of the feng shui beginner. The answers provide fresh solutions to long term problems.

Health

It seems a curious notion that the position of our furniture can be harmful to health. Yet feng shui is based on sound reasoning which backs up such an argument.

With perfect feng shui the natural energy of the environment works for you and you reap the benefits, which extend to enjoying new vitality. If your house and its contents are in opposition to the principles of feng shui then you are being undermined on a daily level and your health will certainly suffer. With feng shui you can live and work in a healthy environment. Feng shui cannot provide a cure-all. However, those with inner strength derived from feng shui are less likely to succumb to illness. The pa kua direction related to health is the east so, for those suffering ill-health, that is the area that needs stimulation.

Can feng shui cure ill health?

Often feng shui can diagnose problems which cause ill health. Overhead beams are frequently responsible for headaches. A main entrance which runs straight into a kitchen or bathroom can cause nagging health problems as can long, narrow corridors where energy is constricted. Use remedies to counter the effects, including screens, fabric, mirrors or windchimes. Also, make use of the garden. Find the east-facing sector which influences

RIGHT: Look outside in the garden to create feng shui remedies for health problems.

health and put in tall, luxuriant plants – bamboo comes well-recommended – or even a water feature. Avoid thorny roses and red or orange flowering bushes as these will deplete energy. If the sector is already occupied by a metal conservatory try painting it green or black and use fabric to shield the effects of the metal. Put bamboo plants in the east of living rooms. Ensure your environment supports you as much as possible.

EXAMPLE

Three women working in the same office all suffered with stomach problems. The door of their office opened up into a kitchen area dominated by a sink which was polluting energy as it entered the office. After a visit from a feng shui consultant a screen was installed blocking off the sink and the health of all the women dramatically improved as the symptoms faded.

BELOW: Beams are believed to be an oppressive force in feng shui terms, generating disharmony.

Relationships

For those wishing to bring a new relationship into their lives the key sector on the feng shui compass is the southwest. This is the area to nurture and strengthen, with its earth qualities and sunny hues.

Pause for a moment to consider why relationships have been hard to come by and keep. Is it because you are too wrapped up in work? Put a goldfish bowl in the north sector of your living room to harmonise your career prospects. If lack of money is the dilemma then place the goldfish bowl in the southeast instead. While seeking the love of your life it is as well to keep the south of the living room vibrant to improve your social life across the board.

How can feng shui help me find the right partner?

If you are seeking a relationship concentrate on the southwest sector of the building, placing in it

something strong and stable. Try beautiful rocks or crystals or even two tall white candles. A chandelier in the southwest sector of the building would be ideal. Leaving a less grand electric light on in the sector would help to energise it too. Avoid displaying photos there which tie you to your past. Over-sentimentality is not helpful when new relationships are in the offing. The aim is to let the future flow in to your home without hindrance. Plants are also off the agenda here as they destroy the strength of the southwest. If you have a lavatory in the southwest mask its negative energies with a wooden windchime of five rods painted blue or black. For women it is important to ensure the decor of the house is not

RIGHT: A fish bowl is frequently used in feng shui, a moveable solution to numerous problems.

too Yin – or overtly feminine – which will make it difficult for male energy to enter. Keep cumbersome pieces of furniture out of the southwest sector so there is as little pressure as possible exerted upon it.

EXAMPLE

One client of a feng shui consultant discovered that every time she left the light on during the night in the southwest sector of her living room a new romantic association began. Most significantly, it involved a long-time friend who turned into a lover.

LEFT: Cumbersome pieces of furniture, such as this sideboard and shelves, should be sited strategically.

ABOVE AND RIGHT:
A relationship is focused by 'together' pictures and gets extra support when the bed backs on to the wall.

With feng shui many of the problems which arise in a long-term relationship can be tracked back to the bedroom and, fortunately, many of the solutions are simple. When the foot of the bed is looking straight out of the bedroom door there is likely to be conflict. A simple re-arrangement can take away considerable amounts of stress and tension. Choose the pictures on the wall with care. Make sure there's nothing aggressive in the artwork that looks down on the bed. Furnish the south west of the bedroom with a happy photograph of those who occupy the bedroom. In the absence of a portrait which exudes

LEFT: *Put portraits of happy couples in the southwest sector of the bedroom.*

contentment and joy find a picture of another couple for the positive effects will be the same.

Can feng shui improve relationships with my partner?

Ensure you are not sleeping in a bed with two mattresses as that is very divisive. Likewise, a beam running between you and your partner in bed can be catastrophic so if there are beams in the bedroom have them in line with the body below waist level. Put bamboo flutes at either end of beams to counter their negative effects if they cannot be disguised with fabric. It is helpful if there is no toilet or heavy furniture on the floor above the bed causing unnecessary pressure. If there's a bathroom adjoining the bedroom keep the door shut. Ban mirrors from the bedroom as they introduce new people and problems. Put mirrors inside cupboards or cover them at night. Choose a solid headboard for the bed rather than one with bars. Find a picture that reflects your joint goals and place it where it can be seen clearly first thing each morning. Invigorate your romantic southwest sector by burning two candles there at night.

EXAMPLE

After the birth of their first baby, a couple found stress was tearing them apart. On the advice of a feng shui expert they used fabric to curtain off the mirrors in their bedroom which were causing confusion. Their relationship subsequently improved.

A clash between parents and children often occurs when their bedroom doors are adjoining. The energy rushing in and out of both are then on a collision course. If a change of bedrooms is impossible then consider re-hanging one of the doors or judiciously keeping one door closed when the room is not in use. Choose bedroom furniture with curves rather than angles, and bear in mind that large items seem enormous to small children. They dwarf the child and hinder the growth of self-confidence. Pillows bearing vivid imagery can have the same effect. Encourage good sleeping habits in the bedroom by keeping the floor space clear of toys, banning televisions and creating an atmosphere of soft luxuriance using curtains and cushions.

I often quarrel with my children. Can feng shui improve matters?

Strengthen the sense of family in the household by placing a portrait of all its members on the wall at the main entrance where it will become a focal

RIGHT: An atmosphere of comfort in the bedroom will help children develop confidence.

point. Keep the entrance brightly lit. The area linked to relationships with children is the west and placing crystals in that area in the living room, for example, will assist the relationship. If children are belligerent about studying place the crystals in the northeast of the living room, or leave a light on at night there. Should the arguments be caused by personality clashes then keep the light on in the west of the living room. Long corridors can create conflict so invest in some windchimes or wall mirrors.

EXAMPLE

A family sought advice from a feng shui consultant when their teenage son lost interest in schoolwork. The consultant helped his parents to activate the northeast corner of his bedroom and living room, where he was supposed to study, with the use of lights. After three months his relieved parents noticed that, while his ability was not boosted, his level of effort had increased enormously.

BELOW: Keep a happy family photograph in the main hallway of the home where it serves as a constant reminder of togetherness.

Personal Finances

To the untutored eye it seems possible to make your personal fortune merely by putting a bamboo plant in the right spot in the garden. Of course, feng shui cannot be used as some kind of get-rich-quick scheme. Its purpose, however, is to harmonise and through that route it can be utilised to ease unsatisfactory financial crises.

The wealth and prosperity sector of the pa kua is the southeast and it is here that the action will be. On the walls choose pictures of forests, trees or plants or depictions of abundance. Bear in mind that the southeast has wood as its element. In the garden seek to place a pond in the southeast sector and stock it with goldfish if lack of cash is the core of your problems.

My personal finances are in a mess. Can feng shui help?

Buy some Chinese coins, round with square holes through the centre, and keep them in your

RIGHT: Bamboo is a luxuriant, abundant plant often used as a remedy in feng shui.

purse, next to your bank statements and on top of your cheque book as they are powerful energisers. If possible put bells on the inside of doors as these too will stimulate energy through sound. Avoid having anything metal in the southeast sector of the living room or house – so beware of filing cabinets – and don't burn candles there as it destroys the natural energy of wood. Choose wooden furniture above all else, place plants there and perhaps a water feature. In the garden make sure the southeast sector is not a stagnant storage area. If possible make it a *beautiful pond, a home for goldfish which can bring financial success.*

EXAMPLE

A businessman consulted a feng shui specialist after working on the same project for months without success. Using wind chimes the specialist activated the sluggish energy in his wealth and career sectors and within a month he had been promoted. The subsequent increase in pay solved his personal financial difficulties and his project reach fruition.

BELOW: Always include a water feature in the garden – but make sure it does not stagnate. Aim to stock it with goldfish.

Living Rooms

The living room is probably the most important room in the house as this is where family life unfolds. A room suffering bad feng shui will surely have a detrimental effect on the lives of all the occupants.

When the feng shui is beneficial it will likewise enhance the lives of all. Remember it is important for feng shui to enter the living room unhindered and circulate freely. For this to occur it should be possible for you to walk freely around the room without bumping into furniture as your movements will reflect those of incoming ch'i. Generally, square or rectangular rooms have good feng shui. An 'L' shaped room, however is missing an important sector in feng shui terms which affects its balance. This can be remedied by placing mirrors on the inside and a light on the outside, both of which will give the appearance of balance. Wooden floors are welcome in the house as far as feng shui is concerned, as are woollen rugs

RIGHT: Furniture is best placed in an octagonal shape. Seek a natural balance within the room.

or carpets above synthetic ones. Make use of healthy plants with round rather than spikey leaves but don't neglect them. Faded plants cause ch'i to stagnate so be prepared to replace casualties.

What is important about my living room in feng shui terms?

The location of the living room in the house is fundamental. Ideally, it is the room you should first see as you open the front door rather than, say, the bathroom or kitchen. Inside there must be a balance between the amount of wall and window space. As much as we like to have light pouring in it is the solidity of walls which gives those inside the home a sense of security. When you open the door of the living room there should be a wall directly ahead which will contain and settle the energy as it comes in. Avoid blue or red carpets as these will create an unstable foundation in a room which is strongly linked to family energies. A snugly fitting door to seal the room from the rest of the house may be an advantage.

BELOW: *An aquarium is a welcome addition to any room in the house. Use it to activate the energy in a sluggish sector.*

New technology has altered the focus of our lounges. Once the seating would have surrounded the fireplace – the point of heat. Each chair being an equal distance from the comforting, warm blaze, a semi-circle would have been created, a naturally fine feng shui shape. Today it tends to be the television which takes priority with the chairs falling in lines before it. Think about installing the TV in a cupboard to return to a more natural environment. If your suite faces neither fire nor television, at least make sure that it doesn't face a doorway. Now you are getting a feel for feng shui it will come as no surprise to discover that draughts are considered poor form, not least for the discomfort they cause. If the dining area is in the living room choose a round table as they encourage conversation – as well as ch'i – to flow freely. Rectangular tables with husband and wife sitting at either end is a possible source of arguments. A table facing the kitchen door will be subject to excess Yang, causing tempers to flare. Use well-polished

cutlery to facilitate extra ch'i. Keep a wary eye on possible sources of poison arrows and be prepared to disguise them with trailing plants, screens or swathes of fabric.

How can I arrange my living room furniture to fit in with feng shui?

An auspicous arrangement of furniture is in a loosely octagonal shape. Make sure the sofa is placed against a wall. If there is no choice but to site it by a window then use blinds extending to ground level to create a solid backdrop. Choose flat blinds instead of louvres which create shar chi energy. When picking furniture avoid items with low backs or flimsy construction. The aim is to give support to the occupants so solid backrests and arms are the most desirable. Low stools for seating are most undesirable as they create feelings of insecurity. If you have bookshelves ensure they are well lit as this will help dissolve the negative energies from books. Better still, conceal them behind cupboard doors.

Ornamental Items

The light coming into our lives through windows creates mood and controls ch'i. Window dressing becomes crucial as a matter of design and for the purposes of feng shui. Curtains are an obvious choice.

Heavy velvets can help to slow down ch'i which enters too rapidly as it would from a busy road or railway line. Fine weaves are more suitable where the energy is already meandering. Curtains are supremely adaptable and can be full length, half-mast, pelmetted, swagged back or left to fall freely. Permanently drawn curtains made from muslin give a pleasant, dappled light if the afternoon sun is too harsh. All drapes will mask harsh lines which so often surround windows. Blinds are an alternative but avoid slatted blinds which are prone to dispatching poison arrows. The effects of such blinds can be shielded, however, with the use of lightweight curtains. Roller blinds give support to a room and are reminiscent of the uncluttered feel of feng shui. When choosing finials for curtain poles steer clear of hostile arrow shapes and plump for rounded flourishes instead.

What colour curtain fabric is best for my living room windows?

The choice of curtain colour and design is dictated by the elements which govern each

RIGHT: Curtains are adaptable aids to feng shui. Wooden floors are a feng shui bonus.

different direction. That means avoiding red curtains with triangular designs on north-facing windows as this clashes with the water element. Steer clear of green, too, as this will destroy the direction's natural energy. Instead choose shades of blue or purple or wavy designs. Curtains in the east, southeast and south would preferably be green or yellow with strong, upright plant or flower based prints, reflecting the energy of spring bursting forth. For windows in the northwest or west, choose earthy tones including terracotta or silver grey.

BELOW: Book spines are the source of poison arrows. Diffuse them with clever lighting or, better still, keep books behind closed doors.

Lighting forms an integral part of interior design. The vogue for low level lighting has now passed, thank goodness, for pools of darkness do nothing for feng shui. If your house remains shadowy by electric light it may be remedied by nothing more expensive than a new light bulb with increased wattage. Smart use of mirrors in corners can also maximise use of light but choose a large, whole mirror rather than mirror tiles which reflect broken images. If the mirror reflects the food on the table then it symbolises a doubling of wealth.

Are there any ornaments or other additions I can introduce to make the most of feng shui?

Works of art can transform the feng shui of a room but choose pictures with care. Don't plump for depictions of tigers and dragons as these can be most detrimental. You want 'friendly' art with pictures of fruit or plants especially beneficial on a southeasterly wall.

Choose pictures of the sunrise rather than sunsets, or pictures with a sense of water. Pictures on a northwest wall are particularly potent. Place luscious indoor plants in the east and southeast of the room as these will help deflect negative energies. Consider indoor bamboo or orange plants, or jade plants which are linked to money. Avoid spikey-leaved plants like cactus. Put a globe in the north west of the living room to enhance male success. A large urn nearby will help to collect good luck.

EXAMPLE

A man worked 60 hours a week in his office but found nothing paid off. He re-designed his living room following feng shui rules. Within a month the people who were causing him problems at work left or were sacked, he won promotion and clinched an important deal.

OPPOSITE: Large urns are thought to harbour good luck.

LEFT: Choose sympathetic art in preference to the fierce, frightening, stark or violent.

The Kitchen

As advertising executives have long known, the most appealing kitchens are those which smell fresh, look clean and enjoy the benefits of big windows and plenty of light. This falls in nicely with the received wisdom on good feng shui for the kitchen.

OPPOSITE: Clean, clear kitchens with wooden cupboards are fortuitous. Keep ovens and sinks, with their conflicting energies, apart.

In practice it is not so easy to keep a kitchen pristine. However, there are a few shortcuts which invite ch'i inside. Is your larder cluttered by packaged food which has long passed its sell-by date? Are there tins or jars of items that you neither like nor plan to eat? Do yourself a favour and dispose of them now.

The doorway to the kitchen should not be directly apparent from the front door, nor should the cook stand for long periods with his or her back to a door. This perpetuates feelings of insecurity and stresses the cook. One solution is to place a mirror or shiny, stainless steel plate above the hob to provide a rear view. Preferably there should only be one door, in order that the ch'i lingers a while.

An oven has particular significance in feng shui as it is the item which provides the family with its food and so is the key to health. The most auspicious ovens are gas cookers and the least favoured are microwaves, as they lack the focal point of flame. If possible, site the oven on a southeasterly wall, out of alignment with the kitchen door and not beneath a window, which could prompt the family wealth to evaporate into thin air. Wooden kitchen cupboards are fortuitous, as wood supports fire.

Of course, ovens are firmly in the category of Fire as far as the five elements are concerned. Basins, meanwhile, are governed by water, and as water douses fire it is best to maintain a healthy distance between stove and sink. They do not sit happily side by side – allow at least half a metre (20 inches) between the two, or opposite one another. The collision of energies is otherwise reflected in a clash of personalities.

Keep the sink clean and the drains sweet-smelling, both for hygiene purposes and to protect your finances.

Knives send out cutting ch'i, so never leave the blades on display. Keep them hidden in a drawer where they cannot damage relationships. The kitchen is the heart of the home and deserves the best protection from poison arrows that you can afford.

RIGHT: Gas is the most auspicious choice in the kitchen with its similarity to the governing element of fire.

The Bathroom

The days of the outside toilet are all but over. Yet there is much to be said for the old tradition, as far as feng shui is concerned. A toilet is something of a feng shui hazard. Flush it and great amounts of ch'i, quite literally, go down the drain.

This is not such an absurd notion as it may first appear. Each flush generates a vortex that drags down any reserves of ch'i which may have accrued. The answer is to keep the toilet lid down before flushing, and indeed at all times when the toilet is not in use. It is as well to keep the door of the toilet or bathroom shut, too.

Bathrooms and toilets are strongly linked to the element of water. Accordingly they should never be sited in the vicinity of the kitchen, where they could clash with the fire element. Nor should the toilet be next to or opposite the front door, as it could swallow up the entering ch'i before it has had the opportunity to circulate.

Those home improvers who have turned an understairs cupboard into a toilet have made a gross error of judgement, as far as feng shui goes. A toilet at the centre of the house is quite the worst position in terms of finance and health. Try to disguise it by placing a full length mirror on the outside of the door.

RIGHT: Bathrooms are governed by the water element and should be well away from the kitchen.

Mirrors have their part to play inside the bathroom, as well as out. Most of us place a mirror above the sink in the bathroom and that's where we usually catch the first glimpse of ourselves in the morning. Don't underestimate its importance. A view that is shiny and well-illuminated gives you a more inspiring picture than one that is grubby, into which you have to peer and squint. Nor is it beneficial to see oneself divided by a cupboard with two mirrored doors. It leaves a shattered impression.

Once again, the bathroom and toilet should be kept sparklingly clean, a rule of thumb applauded as much by health inspectors as by feng shui experts.

ABOVE: Sparkling bathrooms enjoy good feng shui. Pick a substantial bathroom mirror which will offer a full-face reflection.

Your Bedroom

For hours we slumber in the bedroom in the hope of recharging ourselves with sufficient energy for the day ahead. If any room needs good feng shui, it is this one. First consider where the bedroom is located. It should be as far from the front door as is practical, to enhance feelings of security. Disturbed sleep is, by any standards, a sure way to jeopardise the day. Badly placed mirrors, poorly sited beds and a clutter of clothes could contribute to that lack of rest which makes us fractious and ill-tempered. Sleeping in an alcove or with shelves and books above your head can reduce the beneficial power of sleep

BELOW: Conceal mirrors in the closet to enjoy the full benefits of a good night's sleep.

Ensure that your bed is well-supported at its head by either a wall or firmly attached headboard. Position it out of alignment with the doorway or risk the effects of shar ch'i cutting across it. If the bedroom is beamed, consider the luxury of a four-poster to protect yourself from oppressively poisoned arrows.

From the bed the occupants should have a good view of the door – but not of their reflection in a mirror. This can have a devastatingly draining effect. Why not eliminate the problem by concealing a mirror on the inside of a wardrobe door?

The space beneath the bed should be kept clear. Resist the temptation to use it for storage, for it presents an important channel for ch'i.

If a bathroom or toilet adjoins the bedroom keep the door firmly shut at night. Consign all electrical items, like computers, hi-fis and computers, to alternative rooms to rule out the risk of electro-magnetic pollution.

As far as wall decorations go, why not pick a picture that reflects your hopes and aspirations. It could be a picture of exotic India or an endearing portrait of a child. To wake up and be confronted with an image of your ambitions provides an inspirational focus.

Should you want to introduce a little romance into your life, why not put a vase of fresh red or pink flowers near the bedside?

BELOW: Allow for spaces above and below the bed to ensure the free flow of ch'i.

EXAMPLE

A man was concerned that his girlfriend never had enough time for him. His bedroom was decorated with pictures depicting the horrors of war and death. Neither of them realised that this was a prime source of problems. When the illustrations were removed the atmosphere of the room immediately improved and so did the relationship. Afterwards the couple got engaged.

Bedrooms for Children and the Elderly

Children are resilient little souls and as such they are less prone to the effects of bad feng shui. Nevertheless, it would be wise to ensure they do not sleep beneath beams or overhanging features in a bedroom, including shelves and cupboards. If your child is young enough to appreciate a mobile, hang it over their feet instead of their head.

In matters of taste, children frequently clash with their parents. Feng shui may give adults the advantage here, for each gruesome warrior or monster picture that is stuck to the walls should be counterbalanced with something altogether more peaceable and positive. In doing so, remember that it is beneficial for a child to express his or her identity in the bedroom, as this lays the foundation for a stronger character.

RIGHT: Choose squat furniture so youngsters are not dwarfed. Let children express themselves in decoration.

Place the headboard against a wall, rather than a window, to soothe a niggly nature. Beware of bunk beds, as the child sleeping below feels claustrophobic, while the one above is left riddled with insecurities. One answer is to regularly change occupancy of the beds.

Ancestor worship has always been a major feature of the Chinese way, so it stands to reason that care of the elderly is also of paramount importance. People also feel their own happiness is bound up with those in the previous generation (indeed, in several earlier generations), which lends added impetus to the task of caring for the aged.

The key to twilight bliss is to instil a sense of security so that the older person is not burdened by fear of sickness or violence. While senior citizens may appreciate the energy generated by the rising sun in the east, they will feel more at home out of the harsh light in the mellow westerly directions. Inject extra strength with the use of powerfully coloured bath towels.

Make good use of bird baths and tables within view from the window to offer visual stimulation and an important link to nature. Encourage older people to display photos of their existing families, rather than sepia prints from the past.

LEFT: Injections of strong colours can bring vitality to the elderly.

The Front Door

Through this, the mouth of the house, comes ch'i. Accordingly it is vital that the front door gives a warm welcome by being an appropriate size and shape, bigger than the rest of the doors in the house and inwardly opening. It should be solid and snugly fitting.

A small front door will leave the occupants fractious with one another. A tatty front door with chipped paint and cracked glass panes is also far from ideal. Shiny door furniture invites money inside.

While ornaments or plants to the side of the house are fine, don't allow anything to obstruct the door, its view and the ch'i that flows through. All such obstructions effectively limit potential opportunities. A door that sticks or is prevented from fully opening by boots and coats behind it prevents the optimum amount of ch'i from entering.

Make sure your house is clearly identified, for this leads to better career prospects. Numbers have special significance for the Chinese and the number eight is sought after for its associations with material wealth and good luck. Should you have two digits in your house number, place the second slightly higher than the first to give an uplifting feel to the house. If your house has a name, ensure that it is suitably optimistic and welcoming.

The colour red is auspicious, according to Chinese lore. It speaks of passion, happiness, expansion and energy. If your house has whitewashed exterior walls, red is the ideal choice for the door paint. Should the house be made of red bricks, think again – too much red could result in feverish behaviour.

It is an oriental custom to remove shoes at the door. This has practical advantages in that mud is not traipsed around the house, but equally the shoes may have picked up energy that is unwanted in the house.

Should the front door lie directly in front of the back door, valuable ch'i will rush through the house, without lingering to pool its energy in the different rooms.

BELOW: Leave shoes at the front door for they can bring unwelcome energies into the household.

OPPOSITE: A solid, well-fitting front door, freshly painted with shiny door furniture is feng shui perfection.

Stairs and Hallways

Some houses have a front door which opens on to the stairs. Valuable ch'i is funnelled away before it can fully circulate. In feng shui terms, such poor positioning indicates financial difficulties. Rebuilding the staircase is not the answer. Perhaps the most drastic piece of house-remodelling would be to re-hang the door. But before even that, try putting a plant between door and stairs and hanging a wind chime above the plant which will both redistribute ch'i.

BELOW: Ch'i will rush up staircases opposite doorways. Place plants strategically to encourage energy to circulate.

ccording to the Chinese, odd numbers signify better luck than even, so it is better to have nine, 11 or even 13 stairs in the home than 10 or 12. To facilitate the flow of ch'i the stairs should be solid rather than slatted. While curving staircases are conducive to good feng shui, spiral staircases are too abrupt.

Keep hallways clear so that the ch'i can flow at a steady pace. If it courses too fast along hallways it creates an atmosphere of tension. Should it meander too slowly the residents are left weary and worn.

What will happen if the room doesn't follow feng shui principles?

If you don't have energy at home which is meandering and friendly the ill effects will become apparent somewhere in your life – not necessarily on the domestic front. Feng shui represents a third of your luck and, as such, it will affect health, career or relationships. Without good feng shui a sense that all is not well will prevail making you feel uncomfortable. Feng shui taps into the unseen energies around you and brings about the strength and support which will help you tackle new challenges and achieve higher ambitions.

BELOW: *Spiral staircases curve too sharply to conduct ch'i.*

Gardens

By definition, water is an integral part of feng shui. Its vitality is never put to better use than in the garden – according to the Chinese, a plot without water is one without life. Water is, after all, a home for frogs and toads which keep the surrounding territory clear of pests. It can soothe jangled nerves, for gently flowing water positively radiates ch'i. The key is in the movement, however, as a raging river whisks ch'i away before its benefits can be felt and a stagnant pond leaves ch'i dead in the water.

OPPOSITE: Koi carp are often used in Eastern ponds to add life and luck to a garden.

BELOW: Oriental gardeners prefer a few well-placed boulders and some subtle spirals to a profuse 'cottage' garden.

Consult the pa kua to discover the most advantageous direction for a new pond. Generally such an addition acts as a stimulant so wealth, health and career sectors might deserve consideration. Fish are highly thought of in Chinese culture. Seize the opportunity to have these lucky icons in the new pond. Once again, odd numbers are deemed the most fortunate, with eight red or golden fish and one black fish a frequent choice.

A garden path should resemble a stream, meandering in gentle curves between its start and end. Straight paths see the ch'i whistling through, without pausing to assist the householder. Avoid spiralling paths which mimic the outline of snakes, as this inspires unwelcome visitors. Paths coming from the west are best if they undulate and curve to counter shar ch'i from the direction of the white tiger. The preferred shape for patios is circular or octagonal, reflecting the shape of the pa kua. Regular patterns are fine for paved areas like this, but steer clear of tessellations which result in straight lines as this is bad feng shui. It is probably best not to site the patio in the wealth sector of the pa kua – a measure of idleness here would never do. Yet it may be an asset in the relationships corner, as sitting on a patio is a companionable pastime. That same old feng shui standard of 'no clutter' still holds good. A patio bordered with rubbish, broken pots and long-dead plants is not conducive to a good flow of ch'i, nor is a path scattered with debris.

ABOVE: Avoid planting red flowers in the east sector of the garden as it could prove harmful to health.

entirely wild. This attracts wildlife, including bees and butterflies which are sought after in the feng shui garden.

The use of statuary has long been a familiar feature of Chinese gardens, and not for aesthetic purposes alone. Their purpose is to keep good luck in and intruders out. If you invest in statues be sure that they are in proportion to the house

In the Orient drifts of garishly coloured flowers are rarely seen. Instead the Chinese use a few plants with enormous flourish. For them, gardens are akin to three-dimensional art forms. Gardeners seek balance between foliage and flowers, shape and scent – fragrant flora encourage ch'i and discourage shar ch'i. The shapes and colours of a garden can be used to mirror the five elements. Fire is represented by bold red flowers and is also reflected in conical shapes. Earth is associated with square or rectangular shapes and yellow blooms, while metal is circular, oval or arched in the colours of silver and white. Water has free form and dark tones, and wood is linked to columns and greens and blues.

Among the flowers most likely to find a place in the Oriental flower bed are chrysanthemums, magnolias, lilies, peonies, narcissi and jasmine. The Chinese are likely to choose indigenous plants and are partial to evergreens.

If one part of the garden is manicured and cultivated, the ideal is to leave another part and do not draw unwarranted attention to the property. The Chinese have an affinity with items like follies and bridges which assume deep symbolic significance for householders. One of the Eastern gardening habits, now widely used in the west, is the inclusion of stones. Most Chinese have an arrangement of rocks in their backyard. The boulders merit selection for their shape or possibly their texture. With feng shui in mind, we can see how stones add Yang solidity to the Yin softness of plants and soil.

For successful feng shui, be even-handed in your approach and don't allow one feature of the garden to overwhelm the rest.

BELOW: Water is a home for wildlife. Water lilies provide a pleasing balance between foliage and flower.

Buying and Selling

Even elementary understanding of feng shui assists in assessing the situation of a new house. In accordance with the Form school of feng shui, look for the green dragon in the west or at the left and the white tiger in the east or at the right. Today we don't expect hills and streams all around. Look for a large building as a dragon, a flatter area instead of a tiger. A road replaces the stream and a tall building the rear hill.

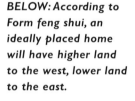

BELOW: *According to Form feng shui, an ideally placed home will have higher land to the west, lower land to the east.*

Always seek to have this 'hill' behind your property rather than in front, where it can give you symbolic support. Homes facing hills never enjoy good feng, as they are immediately thrust into the realms of confrontation.

Houses that face T-junctions are not on auspicious sites, nor are those at the dip of a crescent or next to a busy thoroughfare. There's a possible threat to health for those who live facing either a gap between houses across the street or someone else's home extension. Properties on an S-bend, however, enjoy beneficial ch'i and, broadly speaking, so do those facing south or southeast.

A home that has seen an unhappy marriage dissolved by divorce, redundancy followed by hard times or premature death is unlikely to have good feng shui. Make inquiries about the recent social history of the house to get a measure of its ch'i potential.

Choose a house with a roof that is in proportion to its size. A pyramid roof is inauspicious, given that shape's close links with death. Likewise, a roof which extends virtually to ground level is a feng shui no-no. A blue roof reflects water on top of a mountain and could lead to misfortune. Use bamboo flutes as a remedy.

Given your birth details, a feng shui consultant will be able to advise on the most advantageous date for moving home.

BELOW: Check up on the recent history of the house to discover whether it is likely to possess good feng shui.

FENG SHUI IN THE OFFICE

The office is the venue for decision making and therefore a place for contemplative thought and focus. Given good feng shui, the resolutions made there will be fortuitous and its occupier will reap long-term benefits and rewards. Bad feng shui could have implications for finances, casting a shadow over future prospects.

It is at work that we tend to accumulate frustrations and scores of minor irritations that crank up the stress levels. Feng shui practitioners aim to remove as many of the petty woes as possible to make daily chores a far more pleasant and productive experience. Increasingly, employers are realising that investment in simple feng shui solutions is money well spent.

Much of the feng shui that applies to businesses appears to be stating the obvious. This is the common sense element rearing its head again. Feng shui helps not only by harnessing earth energy, but by making people stop, think, re-evaluate and orchestrate a well-ordered approach.

Office Furniture

Siting the office desk is of paramount importance. This is the place many workers spend hours of their day hoping their efforts will increase the wealth and efficiency of the business. Good feng shui lends important advantages. The desk should be in a commanding position in the room, that is, in sight of but not in the line of the door. With the desk in this position the occupier enjoys a feeling of authority and inspires respect. Those who sit with their backs towards the door are subject to feelings of paranoia and their esteem is undermined.

OPPOSITE: At a cluttered desk it takes twice as long to get work done.

BELOW: Crystals are a useful feng shui tool.

There should be more space in front of the desk than behind it. Ensure that poison arrows aren't aimed at you from pointed furniture behind your desk. The desk itself should observe the first basic rule of feng shui. It should be kept free of clutter, for a clear desktop leads to increased clarity of vision regarding work projects. Conversely, a desktop laden with bills, correspondence and yesterday's sandwich wrapper is continually distracting and its user is perpetually unfocused.

What is the best way to furnish my office?

Avoid glass desks as these render no support and create weak foundations. Beware of pillars in the office which are wholly negative. Veil their effect by placing plants around them. You may find the plants ail quickly and need replacing but never mind. It is better the plants get ill instead of you. Make sure you are backed up with solid furniture, including a sturdy, high-backed chair. Sit with a wall behind you. Only sit with your back towards a window if there is a tall building just beyond which can act supportively. Place a giant urn in the southwest area to collect some luck and instil some stability and solidity there with the use of rocks and crystals. Pin up a picture of someone who inspires you which will introduce helpful people to your life. The aim is to create a vibrant atmosphere which is Yang rather than Yin, combining both a sense of fun and a feeling of achievement and ambition.

EXAMPLE

A woman working from home was in the firing line from the door, a metal filing cabinet behind her and a curved desk in front. After re-organising her office in accordance with feng shui her business was quickly re-vamped and a variety of long-term projects came to fruition unexpectedly quickly.

Working Relationships

At work we seek the support of colleagues. Use feng shui to help win that vital prop. It helps to have a desk that is amply sized, as a small area is quickly filled. Wooden desks decorated with red flowers are considered most auspicious, but don't forget to replace the blooms as soon as they begin to wilt.

Make sure all four desk legs are firmly on the floor. A wobbly desk could lead to instability at work. Consider your goals and put an illustration of them on the wall opposite your desk to act as a reminder. Try laying the pa kua over the desktop to see where items are best placed. Put the photo of the children in the family sector, the petty cash in the wealth sector, in the knowledge sector put reference books, dictionaries and computer discs, and keep your computer in the career sector. These are not hard and fast rules but simply indicate how to use feng shui at work. Be aware that computers, cables and other electrical paraphernalia are considered a fire energy. If there's an excess of 'fire' in your office control it by introducing a water feature.

Are there any feng shui tips to help combat harrassment at work?

Avoid the office at the end of a long corridor. If there's no escape from using it invest in mirrors for the corridor walls to calm the fast-moving chi. Always make sure that you sit where you can see the door. If this is not possible, position a mirror so you can at least see its reflection. This will reduce a feeling of paranoia. Check that the lighting in the office is sufficiently bright. Harsh lights are draining on the nervous system, while soft lighting is a strain on the eyes. Never sit under a beam or sloping roof.

EXAMPLE

A bank boss was concerned about the lack of support he received from members of staff. Concerned at his exposed office which was mostly glass, a feng shui expert put in blinds to improve support, moved his desk, installed a querin to deflect shar chi from a nearby building and popped a model of a tortoise in a north-facing cupboard. Soon he reported that persistent headaches had lifted, staff were being more co-operative and arguments had diminished.

LEFT: Place a pa kua over your desk then arrange it in accordance with feng shui.

Dealing with the Boss

The root of an employee's personal success at work lies with self-confidence. Those who have faith in themselves and their ability have nothing to fear from a fellow worker, be it a boss or an underling. It is important to have good feng shui at home and in the office. Both places should offer you a sense of protection on a daily basis and from this you will gain self-confidence.

Feng shui consultant Rénuka has found that the lives of all her clients have improved after following feng shui advice. 'Although people are at first reluctant to pay for a service they cannot see, fortunately everyone experiences their lives becoming easier. They get a sense of flow and they benefit from keeping within that stream. It runs neither too fast nor too slow. They have fewer anxieties and more inner confidence.' Only one person has reported a sense of everything staying the same after consulting Rénuka. This was probably because she failed to follow the feng shui tips closely enough.

BELOW: A terrapin kept as a pet in the north of the garden, or a stone ornament of a tortoise, will help build self-confidence.

I'm scared of my boss. How can feng shui make my life easier?

When you meet the boss, position yourself so you reap the feng shui advantage. Have a solid wall behind you and keep the door within your sights. If possible, don't have a desk between you as that is confrontational, with the power in the hands of the desk-owner. Never sit with your back to a spikey plant during important meetings. Activate the northwest sector of the office with a metal wind chime – but avoid putting plants there. If possible, keep a terrapin in the north sector of your garden. This will lend inner fortitude and increase self-confidence.

LEFT: Never sit in front of a spiky plant which sends out poison arrows.

Starting a New Business

Planning to open a new shop or business? Don't forget the basic feng shui concepts that govern fortuitous sites. Look for a mountain or large building behind the site, a dragon or large building to the left, a tiger or smaller building to the right, and a river or road in front. Bear in mind, too, the path of shar ch'i and its prevalence around T-junctions, near pylons, along straight roads and so forth.

OPPOSITE: Start a new business in a thriving area which shows no sign of decline.

BELOW: Plants can be useful conveyors of vibrancy in an office.

Check out the neighbourhood and the fate of previous occupants of the premises. If other businesses are doing well and the occupier progressed to a bigger outlet, then all well and good. Alarm bells should sound, however, if there are signs of decline in the vicinity and the previous business went bankrupt.

Use the pa kua for assistance when deciding where to site the boss's office, staff room and cash till. The head of a business should be afforded an office as far from the main entrance as is practical. It should not be a thoroughfare but something of a sanctuary where a manager has time to consider the overview before reaching a conclusion. Avoid having a lavatory positioned above the accounts section. In restaurants it is fortuitous for the kitchen to face south or east.

If the office is in a block its corridors may warrant special attention. Ch'i moves rapidly down long, thin, unbroken corridors, leaving workers feeling drained. Remedies here include chimes and pot plants which disrupt the course of the ch'i.

As large pieces of electrical equipment are frequently found in offices today, metal is best placed on a westerly wall, corresponding with its element. However, some companies may feel their machinery should be fitted securely in the wealth zone of the pa kua to stimulate growth.

Machinery like this is not all good news, however. Not only are their box shapes capable of sending out poison arrows from sharp edges, but they are also perceived to exude electrical pollution. The answer is to install big, green plants to counteract these effects, one for each major electrical item.

Useful Tips

Businesses can capitalise on feng shui when they design their reception area. This is the public face of an otherwise private enterprise and it needs to be warmly welcoming to beckon new business inside and thus generate good fortune. Through the reception area comes the ch'i which can make a business vibrant. It inspires visitors and workers alike.

BELOW: Create an ambience with some well-placed candles and flowers.

W ithout an inflow of energy there's a danger of lethargy setting in among staff and in general trade. Properly arranged, the reception can maintain the flow of ch'i which will carry a business to further success. In feng shui terms it is far more important that the reception is suitably furnished than, say, the rarely seen executive suite. It is advisable to divorce the roles of receptionist and switchboard operator. Visitors will find it most distracting to be confronted with a person who is perpetually on the telephone. The switchboard area should be away from the public's gaze. The seating area should be comfortable and inspire feelings of security. Flimsy plastic or metal-framed chairs are far from ideal. Receptionist and visitor should be shielded from the direct line of the door through which winds will blast and render them uncomfortable. Low-lying tables can provide the form feng shui equivalent of a tortoise which lends stability. Plants in the south, southeast or northwest will prove helpful, stimluating the wealth, recognition and networking sectors of the pa kua.

In the office itself avoid partition walls which can curtail creative thinking. Managers who are not in separate offices should occupy the corner of a room facing outwards so they can better monitor progress in the office. They should have a wall or at the very least a screen behind them. Taking a break outside the office is likely to rejuvenate a worker, as is a drink of bottled water. Relaxation exercises are equally beneficial. Such measures should be built into office routine.

LEFT: Reception areas are the public face of a business and should be warm and welcoming.

Stress Busters

A constantly ringing telephone is a sure way to set tension rising. One remedy is to place a heavy stone next to the phone, reducing the energy in that immediate area. On the other hand, if lack of calls is presenting a dilemma, hang a crystal above the telephone to improve the flow of ch'i.

OPPOSITE: More employers than ever before use feng shui to get the best out of people in the workplace.

BELOW: Bring down stress levels by keeping work stations tidy.

Lighting is another prime source of stress at work. Low-level illumination that makes it difficult to see things properly induces a feeling of inadequacy. Lights that give off a strong glare, like strip lighting, are equally detrimental. Remove a nagging frustration by ensuring your desk area has sufficient brightness to supplement background lighting; a spot lamp is ideal.

Keep storage items at a low level to avoid the anxiety of pressure bearing down around your head, the fullest shelf should be the lowest. Beware the poison arrows from books and folders and choose shelving with doors.

Give an illusion of refreshing space in cramped offices by putting up landscape paintings and photographs.

When offices are shared it is never a good idea to directly face a colleague. This head-to-head arrangement tends to lead to confrontation. Always try to screen the space between the two desks – even a computer screen helps – or better still split them up so both face a door.

If an office is filled with numerous desks, have them placed irregularly rather than in rows. Desks in straight lines encourage the speed of ch'i to increase and with it will go the fruits of everyone's labours.

In most busy offices there is someone who will sneak home early. Study the position of his or her desk. Is it within sight of the door? If so, that exit is on their mind all day. To cure the tendency, simply move the desk to a point at which the door is not in view. Employees who suffer above average levels of sickness should have their desk moved to the pa kua health sector (northwest), while those who talk too much should be kept out of the pleasure sector (north).

If you are a worker attending an important meeting with superiors, try and secure the chair facing the door, as it offers a beneficial position.

FENG SHUI DEVICES

The next time you visit a Chinese restaurant, take a long look around. You are likely to see mirrors, large ones which reflect the diners and small ones, perhaps surrounded by the trigrams. Note the use of lighting and candles. There may be an aquarium or fish bowl, possibly in the vicinity of the cash till. Can you hear the trill of wind chimes as you leave? Now you're armed with some degree of knowledge of feng shui, these items which once seemed inconsequential begin to make sense. The eating house is run by someone who observes feng shui and seeks its prescribed remedies to reverse bad luck and deflect ill fortune.

Feng shui 'cures' broadly fall into one of the following categories: mirrors, sound, lighting, crystals, water, life, movement, electricity and colour. This section gives an initial guide on how to use them.

There are important rules to remember, however. Don't overdo it. A house that resounds with the tinkling of numerous wind chimes or gleams with crystals the size of fists is by no means guaranteed good feng shui. Those extreme and extravagant measures are more likely to obliterate the benefits of feng shui entirely.

Having made an addition of, say, a wind chime, remember to monitor changes which occur thereafter with an open mind. A small change may be sufficient as a cure – don't underestimate its potency.

Mirrors and Wind Chimes

The virtues of a mirror are many, according to the Chinese. As a remedy in feng shui they are used to bounce back shar ch'i as it heads towards a property. The one required for the job is the pa kua mirror, which has already been mentioned. It is octagonal, like the pa kua itself, and is surrounded by the eight trigrams positioned in the Earlier Heaven Sequence. If you decide to use such a mirror, be sure to hang it the correct way, that is, with the Yang trigram of three unbroken lines at the top.

A pa kua mirror is intended to be used discreetly. In hanging it, be sure not to deflect shar ch'i onto a neighbouring property, so impeding their feng shui. Angle it upwards so the poison arrows are deflected harmlessly into the air.

Adorning the house with Chinese icons does not come naturally to everyone. The pa kua

RIGHT: Hang mirrors at the right height so you reflect the whole face not just parts of it.

mirror can be substituted for a small convex mirror, or even a highly polished door knocker or handle. Remember, too, that a growing number of feng shui experts deride the 'cure' of hanging pa kua mirrors.

Mirrors are used in Chinese homes when the owners wants something to 'disappear' in feng shui terms. This might be a badly sited lavatory, for example. Once its door is covered with a full length mirror, the Oriental householder is happy in the knowledge that what he cannot see will not hurt him.

A mirror can likewise add depth. If your house is missing a sector because it has an irregular shape, use a mirror to create the illusion that it is really there. Some restaurants install mirrors to create the illusion of twice as many customers.

When you hang the mirror, be certain it reflects the whole image and doesn't chop people off at the neck. Keep mirrors clean and blemish-free, purchasing the best quality you can afford.

Mirrors help to maximise light – and therefore ch'i – in ill-lit rooms. Stagger mirrors along the walls of long corridors to stop ch'i dashing along and wasting itself. But be wary of hanging something reflective close to the front door – it could send ch'i back before it enters the household properly.

Wind chimes, echoing 'feng' or wind are deemed to have a cleansing action, but be sure you like the sound of them before you buy. The superstitious Chinese believed that ghosts and spirits feared the sound of wind chimes. They are made of metal or wood – experts differ on which is the best – and both types stir sluggish ch'i. Hang them high so they don't dangle on people's heads as they pass.

Should wind chimes grate on your nerves, choose bamboo flutes, which should be hung in pairs at an angle so they don't engender poison arrows. Other devices believed to stimulate ch'i are silk banners or flags, mobiles and windmills. Feng shui has adapted with the technological age and endows the television, stereo and video recorder with the ability to stir ch'i.

ABOVE: Wind chimes will stir sluggish ch'i, enabling it to meander around the home.

Candles and Lighting

Lights, which are reminiscent of the fire element, are extremely Yang and, as such, are warmly energising. They are most appropriately placed in the south, southwest and northeast sectors.

There are numerous ways to manipulate the ch'i which emanates from lights. A small, dark hall can have its atmosphere transformed with some bright lights. This uplifting feeling quickly spreads to the rest of the house, as trapped ch'i gets on the move again.

Shady corners, sloping ceilings and recesses can likewise be enlivened with clever lighting. Make use of lights which point upwards wherever possible. Shades and stands can be bought in a wide variety of colours and materials and in all manner of shapes. Choose the softly curving in preference to angular or threatening shapes. Bare light bulbs are a feng shui no-no. Ensure that your shade is sufficiently large to shield the bulb from view.

The effect of electric lights can range from shadowy through subtle to glare. A compromise is the best option, of course, but bear in mind the use to which each room is put.

Rooms buzzing with activity need to be brightly lit to complement the Yang energy. Bedrooms, on the other hand, should be restful; subdued lighting beckons inactive Yin. The installation of a dimmer switch affords the best of both worlds.

Kitchens require a satisfactory level of lighting in all corners of the room. An office, meanwhile, may only need bright illumination in one area. Consider using bulbs which mimic daylight for such a purpose.

Not many of us want or could afford one, but a cut glass crystal chandelier is something of a feng shui bonus. Candles are closer to the mark for most of us and they are also regarded as good feng shui. From candles we receive a soothing glow and they are usually more portable than electrical fittings, so can be taken to the key sectors for enhancement. However, it is worth remembering that the very best ch'i of all comes from the sun.

ABOVE: Recesses such as this can be enlivened with creative uses of lighting, ensuring a smoother flow of ch'i.

OPPOSITE: A cut glass chandelier helps to radiate ch'i around the house.

Crystals, Plants and Water Features

BELOW: Crystals have long been used for the purposes of healing in the East. Now they are becoming fashionable in the West.

For centuries crystals have been used for healing and to improve people's general sense of well-being. It is believed that crystals are one of nature's stores of energy which benefit those in its range. The wearing of specific crystals is once again approaching high fashion.

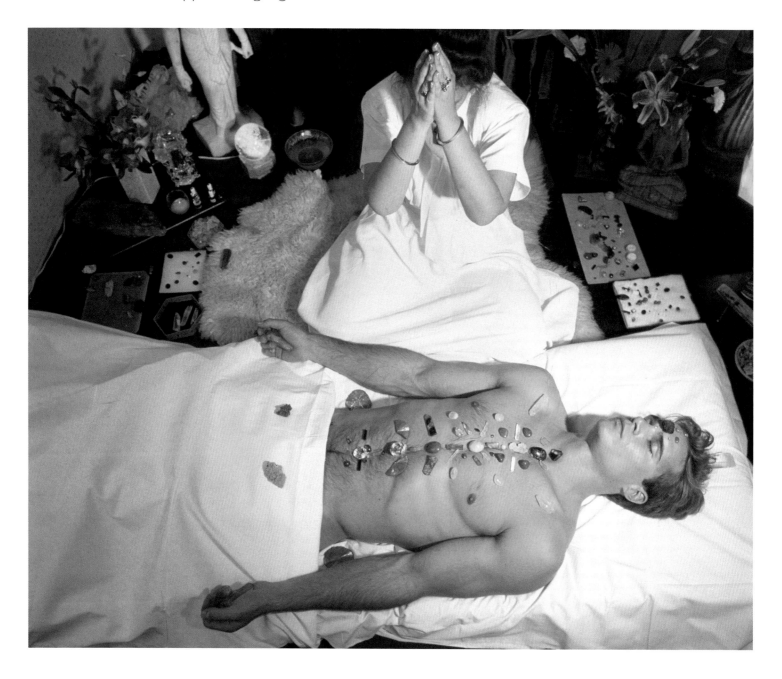

As a feng shui 'cure', crystals are valued for the way they deal with light. Crystals are refractors of light, which means they conjure up the colours of the rainbow when they are captured in the rays of the sun. By this, ch'i is moved around at its optimum pace.

Crystals don't need to be mighty in size to carry out this task. A small crystal is as adequate as a large rock. The important thing is to keep it clean so it can carry out its duties unhindered. Hang crystals in the window, just above eye level so they remain discreet.

Plants and cut flowers represent wood energy, which sits well in the fire-driven south because wood supports fire. Fresh flowers in prime condition are excellent feng shui, but silk flowers are an appropriate alternative. Avoid dried flowers, however, because the faded blooms are associated with dead energy.

A favourite feng shui plant is the Crassula or money tree, a succulent with round or pear-shaped leaves which thrives on little attention (even less in the winter, when it needs little or no water) and is strongly associated with wealth.

Large plants are helpful in the distribution of ch'i but need to be cared for. Signs of decay incur unwanted shar ch'i.

While indoor fountains may be more suited to big businesses rather than homes, there are assorted water features to choose from with some elemental benefits.

Firstly, there's the aquarium containing nine fish – or multiples of nine. If the tank is too small for nine fish, choose another odd number and, once again, avoid the number four. It is important to keep the water clean, as stale water sabotages efforts to instil ch'i.

Table-top fountains are widely available. A bowl of water with floating candles is also equal to the job.

If you remain concerned about stale ch'i, it may be a good idea to place an appealing-looking stone in the offending spot. Keep the stone clean and place it outside in the sunlight at regular intervals to refresh it.

LEFT: A fountain, large or small, will render significant feng shui advantages.

Colours

The belief that colours enhance or inhibit your contentment is nothing new. An army of therapists has made it their job to advise us on the use of colour. It's more than merely colour co-ordination. The blend of hues we choose for the interior of our homes has a telling psychological effect and, for this reason, colour is a feng shui 'cure'.

Already the elements have been assigned a colour. Remember the supportive and destructive cycles associated with the elements. If your marriage is going through a sticky patch, you may want to add fire to support the earth in the southwest sector of your home. A red rug, cushion or chair could be the answer.

In feng shui terms it is ideal to match up element directions with associated colours. That doesn't mean that the north of the house, with its water connections, must be draped in black. An ebony vase, table or even a picture frame is often sufficient to echo the link. White and metallic tones are equally favourable, because metal supports water in the production cycle. Yet it may be as well to keep earth colours (brown and yellow) to a minimum, as earth is destructive for water. Study the cycles closely before deciding on a colour scheme, so you don't inadvertently harm some of your home's naturally occurring advantages.

Outside the elements, there are other principles governing colours. Once again, colours are not right or wrong – it's their effect that counts. Yellow was favoured by the Chinese royalty and was once restricted to the emperor alone. Being the colour of the sun, it is perceived as all powerful. It is also imbued with the qualities of creative knowledge, tolerance and patience.

RIGHT: Too much white in a room is said to muddy the thought processes. Always balance Yang white with Yin black.

White is thought of as pure and innocent in the West. In the East, however, it is the colour of mourning and is used sparingly. Too much white in a room is believed to muddy the thought processes. Always add some dark Yin to counter the busy white Yang.

Team black with pink to imply social advantages. Put it with yellow and you could be the quiz champion of the region. Black is a colour of contradictions. It reflects bruising – children who favour black may be feeling 'bruised' inside – but is also linked to new beginnings.

Red is exceedingly lucky in Chinese terms and as such is the bridal colour. Happiness and warmth are its twin attributes and it roars with energy. Don't splash it all over the walls, though. With red, less is more. Purple is the next best thing. It has strong links to religion and also wealth.

Blue and green are spring colours, broadcasting new growth. Beware of brown, which could lead to stagnation.

LEFT: It is a good idea to check the significance of colours especially when they are combined.

LEFT: In the East people use detailed knowledge of the trigrams and the elements to work out their preferred colours.

Astrology

Feng shui stands alone. It does not involve a belief in astrology, divination and the like. Yet it is frequently mentioned in the same breath as Nine Star Ki, a form of Oriental astrology which looks at energy and time. Like feng shui, it is rooted in the trigrams of the I Ching. It seeks to categorise our lives in cycles lasting nine years, nine months and nine days.

The system originated in Tibet but has been honed in Japan where 'ki' is the translation of 'ch'i'. Supremely detailed, it is another way of making the best of our resources.

Chinese astrology is more familiarly linked to animal signs of rat, ox, tiger, rabbit, dragon, snake, horse, goat, monkey, cock, dog and pig – all representing years. (Remember, when you look up your birth year, that the Chinese new year varies annually and begins in January or February. If your birth date falls immediately prior to the

Chinese new year, remember to assign yourself to the previous year.)

But the horoscopes remain intertwined with feng shui, as you can see. Each has an element attached to it and is either Yin or Yang. The animals further signify a two-hour slot in every 24.

It is the collection of beasts that also form the 12 earthly branches on the feng shui compass. They team up with the 10 Heavenly Stems – chia, yi, ping, ting, wu, chi, keng, hsin, jen and kuei – which each have an associated

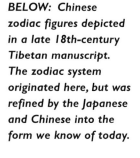

BELOW: Chinese zodiac figures depicted in a late 18th-century Tibetan manuscript. The zodiac system originated here, but was refined by the Japanese and Chinese into the form we know of today.

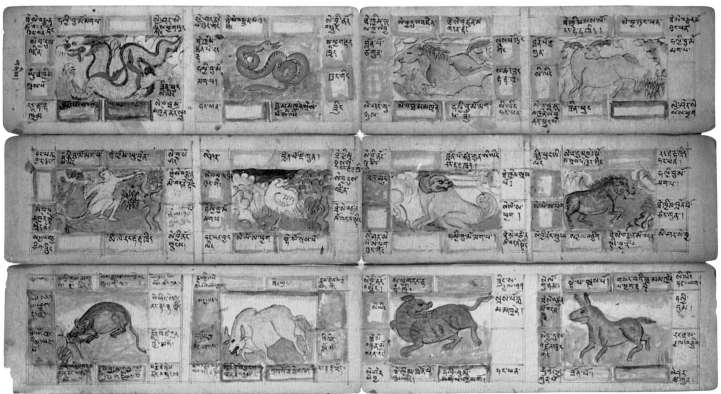

number, planet, compass point, season and element – to become the full 24 directions on the feng shui compass.

All Asian countries have their own slant on horoscopes. Studies have been carried out for centuries and it is difficult to skim the surface without causing confusion.

Central to Chinese culture is the existence and perpetual use of the almanac. This is a book, or table, containing forecasts for the year. Almanacs have been in existence across the globe since antiquity. In the beginning their main purpose was to issue predictions which helped to prepare the populace for catastrophes to come. It also pointed to auspicious days of the year and periods associated with good fortune.

Many almanacs have adapted to survive, first by including astronomical data, then by concentrating on the physical rather than the metaphysical. Yet the Chinese continue to set store by their almanacs, which still focus on the art of soothsaying.

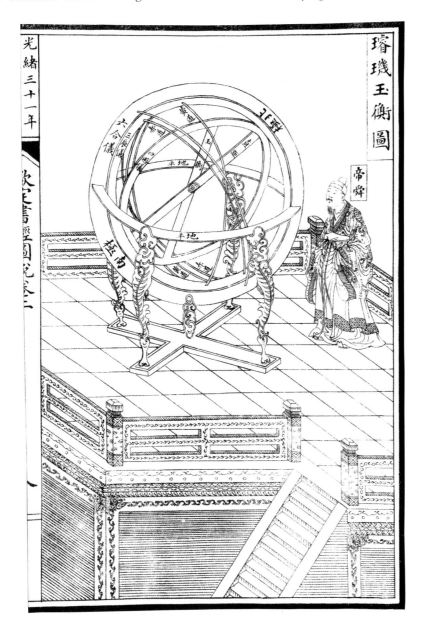

ABOVE: The ancient Chinese were advanced in the arts of astrology and astronomy.

CONCLUSION

As you approach the end of this short tour of feng shui, you will have formed your own opinions on this ancient art. More complex than geomancy, more subtle than interior design, it has a host of aspects which we have only briefly touched upon.

The aim of this book has been to illustrate the 'chain reaction' of feng shui, how one misplaced desk or ill-conceived colour scheme can have a palpable effect.

In the West we tend to lead hectic lives, dashing between work and home, bolting meals, cramming our daily agenda full of appointments. There's precious little time to stop and think. Feng shui helps prompt that re-evaluation, which can transform an unsatisfactory existence into a far more fulfilled life, simply by stopping us swimming against the tide. It is not a magic wand which instantly rights wrongs, so keep it in context and think instead of making the most of your destiny. Used as a route to a more harmonious existence, feng shui becomes a pillar of strength.

Only you can judge the efficacy of feng shui, as it is a highly personal venture. Thousands have been convinced by results they have experienced. Still, it takes a radical overhaul in beliefs for a Westerner to embrace ancient Chinese superstition. As such, it may not come naturally to believe that stone lions guard against burglars or that, correctly placed, a goldfish bowl solves long-term cash-flow problems. Interpretation of ancient texts into modern living has left feng shui riven by divisions about what constitutes genuine and pseudo feng shui.

Allied Arts

The Chinese are not alone in their belief that earth energy can be harnessed and put to good use. In India the equivalent of feng shui is vastushastra, the ancient Hindu science of architecture. Similarly its essence is to engineer a harmonious existence while warding off evil forces.

OPPOSITE: There are many cultures that promote the use of space clearing. The use of light is fundamental to all of them. Whether it be natural light, or as here man-made, one should monitor how it is placed in the home, as this will regulate the flow of positive/negative energy.

It dates back some 5,000 years and featured in the Vedas, the famous scripts of the era. Practitioners use a grid in order to map out paths of energy which reflect the shape of a torso. Legend has it that an unknown being poised to come between Heaven and Earth was grabbed by the gods and laid face down on the ground, where it became human. It is this outline which appears in the grid, called the Vastu Purusha Mandala.

Energy enters a building through the Purusha's head in the northeast, travels down its arms to the southeast and northwest, and ultimately accrues by the feet in the southwest. To invite the greatest amount of energy inside it is important to keep the east, northeast and north directions clear of obstacles. It is in these directions that one should find the greatest number of doors and windows. The direction of the sun also has an important part to play, with the cooler rising sun imbued with more helpful powers than the setting sun.

Like feng shui, vastushastra has enjoyed a new lease of life recently. Indeed, the vogue has put some strain on the Indian national purse, as officials re-model their homes and offices, seeking to win the advantage in India's closely contested political race.

Native cultures have long recognised the perils of dead energy and how it drags down the atmosphere of a space. The term fostered for its removal is space clearing. Although techniques vary the procedure is known among cultures as geographically diverse as the Maoris, Aborigines, Zulus and Hawaiians, and it is most closely associated with the American Indians.

Sometimes bells, or musical instruments including drums or gongs, are used for clearing. Others prefer the use of smoke, which can be distributed with the use of a feather. Another method is to toss salt in the vicinity while praying. With all techniques it is the spiritual awareness that makes the difference, played out in ceremony and ritual.

RIGHT: Native Americans are finding a booming market for their feng shui equivalent, space clearing.

How to find a Feng Shui Consultant

If you have decided, having read this book, that feng shui has the answers you need, the next step is to find a consultant who can deliver a detailed analysis of your home or office.

I t sounds deceptively easy, but like all trends, feng shui has its fair share of hangers-on who will embark on sales talk which is heavy on jargon but featherlight in fact. It falls to you to sift the decent sorts from the opportunists before paying for feng shui advice.

There are few *bona fide* feng shui masters capable of carrying out intuitive inspections, particularly in the West. Although preserving this elite for years kept Confucian order in the practice of feng shui, it has latterly diluted the art. However, there is an abundance of practitioners.

With the knowledge you have gained so far you are poised to challenge bogus consultants with confidence. Always inquire how long they

have been practising feng shui and where and how they trained. It is unlikely that anyone studying feng shui for less than five years has a sufficient grasp of the subject to warrant hard cash.

Be prepared to check out training schemes and teachers that you have been quoted, contacting non-profit-making feng shui societies or institutes for guidance, if necessary. If you still have nagging doubts, ask if you can contact previous clients.

Always inquire whether they know compass feng shui as well as form feng shui. If they do not, seek an alternative who does, for this indicates a deeper grasp of the subject. It will be clear to you already that a competent feng shui consultant needs your date of birth and the construction dates of the building in order to make an evaluation.

Sometimes someone of Oriental name or appearance will insist on more money than a Western counterpart. Scrutinise their training history before being convinced. Likewise, be sceptical of the feng shui 'expert' who prescribes cures which he or she has for sale.

Don't be fooled by time-wasters. It won't take several hours to investigate a small flat. The average-sized house is unlikely to take more than two hours to assess. Expect the experts to charge by the square foot or by the hour.

Ensure that there is a route back to the consultant, either by telephone or follow-up visit, as you may have questions to pose.

OPPOSITE: A home which achieves good feng shui is a pleasure to behold.

BELOW: Some feng shui experts place great emphasis on the position of the planets.

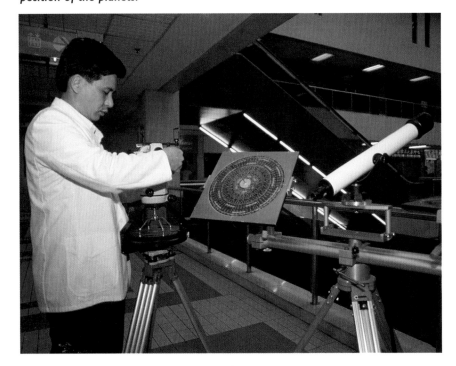

Glossary

Almanac Calendar of predictions or forthcoming events.

Ch'i Earth energy.

Feng Wind.

I Ching The Book of Changes, an ancient text which has been expanded and studied for centuries, central to the art of compass feng shui.

Lo P'an Feng shui compass.

Lo Shu Magic square or cube featuring the numbers one to nine. It is considered magic because in all directions the rows add up to nine.

Pa Kua The Yin-Yang symbol surrounded by eight trigrams.

Poison arrow Unhelpful energy.

Shar ch'i Unhelpful energy.

Shui Water.

Tao The Way, a religious philosophy which dominated in China.

Trigram One of eight symbols composed of three lines, each line broken or solid.

Wen The Green Dragon of form feng shui.

Wu The White Tiger of form feng shui.

Yang Creative energy.

Yin Receptive energy.

Index

Picture credits

The publishers would like to thank the following sources for their kind permission to reproduce the pictures in this book:
Bridgeman Art Library, London/Private Collection, *Chinese priests tossing bamboo tallies to predict the future by William Alexander (1767-1816), pub. by G&W Nichol, London 1800,* 10; Carlton Books 34, 76; Corbis/Peter Aprahamian 81/Richard Cummins 59/Michelle Garrett 72/Eric and David Hosking 26/Wolfgang Kaehler 57/Earl Kowall 92/Douglas Peebles 58/The Purcell Team 1, 79/Arthur Thevenart 4; et archive 6, 12, 17, 43, 87; Mary Evans Picture Library 11t, 14; Werner Forman Archive 11b, 68; Fortean Picture Library 22; Robert Harding Picture Library 20, 27, 29, 35, 41, 45, 47, 48, 51, 53, 54, 55, 56, 84, 85, 90; Image Bank 2, 3, 13, 18, 30, 39, 40, 42, 52, 63, 64, 69, 70, 73; Image Select 8, 86; The Interior Archive/Fritz von der Schulenburg (Architect: Jean Oh) 32, 36, 37, 38, 49, 50, 61, 88; Panos Pictures 91; Thomas Stewart 80; Tony Stone Images 16, 19, 21, 24, 28, 31, 33, 44, 46, 60, 65, 66, 71, 74, 75, 78, 82, 83, 93, 94, 95.

Every effort has been made to acknowledge correctly and contact the source and/copyright holder of each picture, and Carlton Books Limited apologises for any unintentional errors or omissions which will be corrected in future editions of this book.